Success
Delegation
in a week

JEREMY KOURDI

Hodder & Stoughton

A MEMBER OF THE HODDER HEADLINE GROUP

Orders: please contact Bookpoint Ltd, 39 Milton Park, Abingdon, Oxon OX14 4TD.
Telephone: (44) 01235 400414, Fax: (44) 01235 400454. Lines are open from 9.00 -
6.00, Monday to Saturday, with a 24 hour message answering service.
Email address: orders@bookpoint.co.uk

British Library Cataloguing in Publication Data
A catalogue record for this title is available from The British Library

ISBN 0 340 73762 X

First published 1999
Impression number   10 9 8 7 6 5 4 3 2 1
Year   2004 2003 2002 2001 2000 1999

Copyright © 1999 Jeremy Kourdi

Typeset by Multiplex Techniques Ltd, St Mary Cray, Kent.
Printed in Great Britain for Hodder & Stoughton Educational, a division of
Hodder Headline Plc, 338 Euston Road, London NW1 3BH by Cox & Wyman Ltd,
Reading, Berkshire.

the Institute of Management

F O U N D A T I O N

The mission of the Institute of Management (IM) is to promote the art and science of management.

The Institute embraces all levels of management from student to chief executive and supports its own Foundation which provides a unique portfolio of services for all managers, enabling them to develop skills and achieve management excellence.

For information on the various levels and benefits of membership, please contact:

Department HS
Institute of Management
Cottingham Road
Corby
Northants NN17 1TT
Tel: 01536 204222
Fax: 01536 201651

This series is commissioned by the Institute of Management Foundation.

CONTENTS

There has been much written and discussed about the changing role of the manager, yet the most important, defining skill of a manager has remained largely unaltered: the ability to work productively through others. This is true for any manager, at any level, in any organisation. The ability to delegate routinely and effectively is one of the key skills that is fundamental to success.

To delegate effectively you must recognise that certain activities must be yours, while others can be shared, and others relinquished. The activities which you undertake must be those which only you can do, and usually include policy-making and planning, people management, evaluation and conflict resolution.

Learning to delegate may require you to change your approach: to think about your team where previously you may have only considered your own work and tasks. This is the first, and possibly the biggest single step for a manager, but it is essential for success.

The advantages of successful delegation are considerable. The direct benefits are obvious, chiefly greater productivity and better use of resources. However, the indirect benefits are no less significant for you, your organisation and the colleagues to whom you are delegating. These might include: better time management and reduced stress; greater understanding leading to process improvements and innovation; improved decision-making; greater motivation; and reduced staff turnover.

Respect and clarity are essential for successful delegation. Above all, managers should treat others as they would wish to be treated themselves, and this is particularly true when delegating.

As you go through the week you will explore the skills that you need to know to successfully delegate work. Your week is set out like this:

Sunday	What is delegation?
Monday	Preparing to delegate
Tuesday	Matching person and task: delegating with authority
Wednesday	Communicating with clarity
Thursday	Overcoming problems when delegating
Friday	Delegation and other key management skills
Saturday	Delegating for the first time

What is delegation?

Delegation is the act of giving someone the necessary
authority to make decisions and act for us in a specified
area of work. In giving someone else the authority to act on
our behalf we must accept that we are at the same time
giving them the 'right' to be wrong.

If managing is achieving results through people, then all
managers should delegate. We know that managers in
successful companies delegate tasks and responsibilities
right down the line. Yet delegation is often dealt with badly.
Many managers don't delegate, and even more don't do it
very well, causing difficulties to the individuals involved
and to their organisation.

Many of the problems associated with poor delegation are
either a failure to communicate, or an inability to do it
properly. The following attitudes are all too typical:

'I would sooner do it myself'
'They'll only mess it up'
'I don't have time to explain'
'I'll have to watch them like a hawk'
'I tried that once – it was more trouble than it was worth'
'I don't want them to do my job for me'

Most managers complain of an excessive workload, with a
vast amount of work to do in a short period of time.
Learning to delegate is therefore a vital practical skill to
master. Delegation is best seen as a personal skill that must
be mastered, rather than a job task. It is one of the keys to
personal effectiveness, making you and your team more
productive and successful.

The benefits of delegation

There are considerable benefits in delegating work for
everyone involved. It allows decisions to be taken at the
level where the details are known, and it reduces delays in
decision-making – as long as authority is delegated close to
the point of action. There are a number of other key
benefits.

For the organisation there is:

- better use of your time, which is expensive
- an opportunity to develop skills and experience in
  subordinates. This in turn provides motivation in
  individuals through achievement
- full use of your team's skills by really analysing what they
  can do
- the development of trained, competent understudies who
  are ready to step in and provide support when required

For you as the delegator there is:

- relief from routine and less critical tasks, extending your capacity to manage
- more time to stand back from the 'hurly burly' of the present and to think and plan for the future. This includes time to plan to avoid problems – and time to deal with them if they occur!
- better time and stress management as a result

For your team there is:

- increasing confidence that comes from greater competence
- more scope to use different skills, and many more development opportunities
- greater interest, involvement and job satisfaction throughout the team

So effective delegation has many benefits. It ensures performance and improves performance. It develops people and can also motivate them.

Barriers to effective delegation

Delegation has few disadvantages, but in practice many managers find it very difficult. The usual excuses include:

'I can do it better'
'I enjoy doing it'
'It has to be done immediately'
'I don't want to complicate things'
'I want to keep my hand in'
'My boss wants me to do it'

It is important to recognise these for what they are: excuses to justify what you want, not real barriers. However, there are genuine obstacles to delegation and these include:

- understaffing
- confused lines of authority
- the wrong people in the wrong post
- a culture of fear, criticism or blame
- underdeveloped people

In many organisations delegation is too often devalued: many managers find it risky, with little reward attached. You should also recognise that it is harder to delegate if you have poor communication skills, or if there is a lack of trust or resistance to delegation among your team. You may therefore need to consider your own leadership style and how to build up the trust of others around you before starting to delegate.

How well do you delegate?

Here is a short questionnaire to help you find out how well you delegate. It has been designed to help identify your strengths and weaknesses, and areas where improvements can be made. Circle the number that best describes you – the higher the number the more that statement describes you. When you have finished add up the numbers circled and mark your total score.

1	At work, I focus on planning, organising, motivating and controlling, instead of doing tasks that others could do	5	4	3	2	1
2	Each of my team know what I expect of them	5	4	3	2	1
3	I keep people informed and I involve team members in goal-setting, problem-solving and process improvement activities	5	4	3	2	1
4	I carefully consider who to delegate work to, matching person and task	5	4	3	2	1
5	I view delegation as a way of developing the skills of people in my team, and I assign work on this basis	5	4	3	2	1
6	When delegating work I always brief team members fully	5	4	3	2	1
7	If a problem arises I give the person doing the task the opportunity to resolve it themselves	5	4	3	2	1

8	When I delegate work I emphasise the end results, rather than the means to accomplishing them	5	4	3	2	1
9	I support and help team members, but I do not allow them to pass on work for me to do	5	4	3	2	1
10	When I delegate work I agree in advance how I will monitor progress: I don't spy or undermine people	5	4	3	2	1
11	When delegating work I am always positive and confident, showing trust	5	4	3	2	1
12	I always give credit for successes	5	4	3	2	1

Total score _____

A score between 60 and 52 suggests that you are doing well. A score between 51 and 34 indicates that you are getting by, but could probably improve your delegation skills in certain areas. A score below 33 means that you need to make changes.

Key steps in successful delegation

There are a number of key stages in successful delegation:

1 *Preparation* – decide what tasks and responsibilities to delegate.
2 *Match the person's skills to the tasks required* – the skills required should be carefully considered. The level of task should be challenging but appropriate.

3 *Discuss and agree objectives* – all aspects of the task, should be talked through. Having allocated tasks you need to agree targets, objectives, resources, review times and deadlines. (Remember that when setting objectives they should always be **SMART**: Specific, Measurable, Achievable, Results Related (or Realistic) and Time Constrained.)

4 *Provide resources* – sufficient resources, in particular time, should be made available.

5 *Delegate authority* – you must provide the person completing the task with sufficient power and authority to make it happen.

6 *Monitor progress* – progress should be regularly checked without interfering or undermining.

7 *Review and assess overall performance* – this is best done by checking achievements against the original objectives.

We will explore these key elements later in the week, but there are some important points to make at the outset.

Preparation
You must focus on the results that you want to achieve and have clear, precise objectives. This may require careful consideration and planning, possibly discussion with other colleagues, but it is vital for everyone involved that you are clearly focused and can pass this on. You may also need to give some thought to priorities: what should come first? Is the work just piling up on *everyone*? If this is the case then delegation may not be the solution. Always consider the *importance* and *urgency* of the task that you are delegating.

Matching person and task

This is another vitally important aspect and one where delegation can go horribly wrong. In order to delegate effectively we need to be able to identify which of our daily tasks could be tackled by other people. The person who is being required to do the job must understand it and have the personal skills and competence to tackle it, even if it is different, important and challenging.

Agreeing objectives

It is vital that you gain acceptance through two way communication. Be sure to check understanding and gain explicit agreement to your plan.

Provide resources and the appropriate level of authority

Make sure that you provide all the necessary resources, as well as the authority to complete the task, and give all the necessary back-up. Define responsibilities clearly and be there to advise when appropriate. Always follow up your actions, and plan how you will monitor and control events.

Monitor progress

It is worth remembering that delegation without control is abdication. This does not mean interfering when there is no need, but control does mean checking progress: not haphazardly but at pre-planned and specified times. Control also involves verifying that things are on track. The purpose of monitoring and control is to make sure that the delegated task is completed successfully and that the desired results are achieved. The key to monitoring is to ensure that the person completing the task remains accountable.

When to delegate

You should delegate when:

- you cannot allocate sufficient time to your priority tasks, or you have more work than you can effectively carry out yourself
- you want to develop your subordinate
- the job can be done by your subordinate

Delegation tip

It is important to recognise that as a manager you should not wait for difficulties and time pressures to arrive, or for someone else to tell you when to delegate. At some stage you will have to manage through others to achieve success, and the sooner you start the better and easier it will be.

What to delegate

You delegate tasks that you don't need to do yourself. You are not just ridding yourself of difficult, tedious or unrewarding tasks. Neither are you simply trying to make life easier for yourself. Delegation may, in fact, make your life more difficult, but also more rewarding and successful.

You should certainly delegate routine and repetitive tasks which you cannot reasonably be expected to do yourself: and you must then use the time you have gained productively.

You should also delegate specialist tasks to those who have the skills and know-how to do them. You cannot *do* it all yourself, and you cannot be expected to *know* it all yourself. You have to know how to select and use expertise. To do this you need to make it clear what you want from the experts, and ask them to present it to you in a usable way.

You may find it useful to think about your job, listing all of the things you do, and decide:

- what must you do yourself?
- what could others do with my help?
- what could others do better than me?
- what must others do?
- who would you delegate to? and what tasks would you give each person?
- what would you do with the extra time?

Summary

Today we have looked at delegation as a whole and seen
that it brings many benefits to both the subordinate and the
manager. We've also seen the key elements for successful
delegation, and looked at when and what to delegate. The
process remains the same at any level. Having first built up
trust we need to:

- be clear about what to delegate
- match person to task
- communicate clearly and agree objectives
- provide resources
- monitor progress
- review and assess overall performance

Tomorrow we will prepare to delegate: this involves
developing the right approach; planning what to delegate;
and overcoming any obstacles.

Preparing to delegate

There are many reasons why people avoid delegating.
These include a lack of confidence, lack of clarity or focus,
and most significantly a fear that they will not get the
results they want. When preparing to delegate you should
ask four basic questions:

1 Am I ready to delegate?
2 What work can I give to others?
3 What does the job involve?
4 What must I do to ensure that people know what they
   are doing?

There is a lot of hype and mystery built up around
delegating, but by answering these four questions
delegating will become a lot simpler and straightforward.

Developing the right attitudes

Delegating successfully depends on many different factors:
the type of job, the work environment, the experience of the
employee, the timing of the situation, and the degree of
understanding between the manager and team member. A
key element in delegating successfully, and finding a way
through all these different factors, is to develop the right
attitude: it is only then that you are likely to generate the
right attitude in others.

The right attitudes when delegating are *positive* ones. We will be looking at them in this chapter and they include:

- Showing confidence and personal security by letting go
- Showing trust
- Being prepared to take risks and support mistakes
- Being patient
- Obtaining commitment
- Being task oriented

Letting go
Good delegators feel confident in their abilities and position in the organisation and have a positive attitude about delegating. Delegating is viewed as a way of preparing team members to be future managers. Above all, good, confident delegators view it as a means of achieving their own, and the company's, goals. This confidence is necessary because it will help you to have the courage to let

someone else perform a task that you would normally do, while still accepting full responsibility for the results.

Many managers have difficulty letting go because they are afraid that others will do something dreadful that they would never have done themselves. If this is you then you need to remind yourself that:

- you are not the only person capable of doing what you do
- it does not matter if the job is done differently to the way that you would do it, as long as it is done to the required standard
- you will not lose control of your work if you let go of a part of it

Showing trust
When delegating, a good manager needs to trust another person to perform a task for which the manager alone will be held responsible. This requires deep and resilient reserves of trust, on both sides, and a positive attitude from

the start. To develop trust during delegation remember the following six dos and don'ts:

1 *Do back up team members' decisions* – even if you don't agree with them back them up when they need support, and always in front of others. Guiding, coaching and counselling is far more effective when delegating than criticism, negativity and disagreement.

2 *Don't dwell on mistakes* – face it now: they are going to happen and probably will whether you delegate or not! People usually realise when they have made a mistake and you should always try to give the person the opportunity to correct it.

3 *Do be clear about your expectations* – share your expectations with team members in advance.

4 *Don't undermine people* – an important rule at any time and never more so than when delegating. This includes avoiding withholding information or spying on your team. Instead of spying, agree clear guidelines for monitoring progress and then stick to them.

5 *Do be honest and open* – hiding information or your own mistakes, even inadvertently, can cause mistrust or resentment. Share information with team members so that they can perform their job, and be straightforward with them. Don't, for instance, manipulate people with implied rewards or pressure them with guilt. This is really about showing respect and courtesy.

6 *Do examine assumptions* – make sure that you are making the right assumptions. If someone succeeds, or fails, was it as a result of what they did? If they are reluctant to undertake the task is it for a reason you understand, or could it be because of something else?

> *Delegation tip*
>
> Showing someone that you trust them to do the task properly will go a long way to ensuring that it is.

Taking risks and supporting mistakes

The best managers are those that are willing to take risks so as to get things done: they are prepared to stretch resources and make mistakes, and are always willing to accept and learn from failure. What are the alternatives? Do nothing? Achieve less than you are capable of?

You do not want people to make mistakes if they can help it, but inevitably they will happen. It is important that people know that if something goes wrong they can admit it: this establishes a positive attitude and encourages team members not to let you down. If support and a 'no blame' atmosphere is not present then the person doing the work will be cautious, distracted, and may ultimately turn a mistake into a crisis by hiding it from you.

Being patient

When you delegate you should be aware that results take time. Remember:

- allow team members the chance to develop their own judgement by using their own methods
- if a project falls behind schedule make sure that the team member has a plan for getting it back on track – don't panic and take over the project
- allow time to *explain* what is required and *agree* what needs to happen i.e. when you will monitor progress

Obtaining commitment

You need to be certain that when you delegate a task it is being received with commitment; that is to say, the people completing it are interested, willing and able. Ability without willingness and commitment is nothing. Gaining commitment can take time but it is absolutely essential. To obtain commitment you need to persuade people that:

- the task they are completing is necessary and worthwhile, however small
- they have the freedom to decide themselves how to work, as long as the objectives are met
- they have been given the task because they are considered capable of completing it

Being task oriented and keeping control

When delegating, remember to focus on the tasks that are being completed. Remember also that effective delegation means that you need to establish a means of control, including *channels* for reporting progress and problems (consider using review meetings, progress reports), and a *schedule* for when reporting should take place.

If you are unhappy with the amount of feedback and control then do two things: establish additional means for monitoring progress, and tell the team member that you are going to follow up frequently on the project's progress. You don't need to make a big issue out of this, nor should it stop you appearing confident and positive about the final outcome: you're just concerned to make sure it stays on track and you can provide support when needed. This warning and dialogue will help to remove any feelings of interference or meddling.

Planning what to delegate

With the right attitude to delegation, the next stage in the process is deciding what work can and cannot be delegated.

Deciding what to delegate is usually prompted by the realisation that there is far too much to do to give each thing the attention it deserves, or that you will not be able to achieve your goals unless you pass some of your responsibilities to someone else. Whatever the reason, to delegate effectively you must carefully consider *what* work you delegate.

Choosing what to delegate
A good way to decide what can be delegated is to make a list of all the tasks you do, and divide them into four sections:

1 *Tasks you must delegate*

These are the tasks that can quite easily be done by someone else, allowing you to make better use of your time. Often they include:
- tasks you have always done
- tasks that came to you 'by accident', perhaps assigned by a colleague without realising you should delegate them
- tasks you enjoy
- tasks with minimal risk involved

2 *Tasks you should delegate*

These include routine tasks that you may never have considered delegating but which can easily be completed by others. This might include tasks that in the past could only have been done by you but now can be done by members of your team.

3 *Tasks you can delegate*

These are tasks that could be completed by others if they had the necessary skills. Delegating these tasks can help your team members to develop the required skills, but it is important to provide the necessary training and support first.

4 *Tasks you must retain*

These are the jobs that are the manager's core responsibilities. They include planning, people management and other major issues (see *What to avoid delegating* below).

It is certainly worth considering where tasks come from and how you deal with them. Many managers take on the work simply because it comes to them, or because they want to do it, without considering whether it can be successfully completed by someone else. A successful manager will delegate as many as possible of the right tasks, and it is worth getting into the habit of considering whether a task can be delegated as soon as it occurs.

Types of task to delegate include:

Recurring tasks
Where a job is likely to recur it is usually best to delegate it to someone who becomes an expert on that activity, handling it faster and more efficiently. If the task is boring, unpleasant or needs to be done repeatedly over a long period then it is best to rotate the responsibility to other individuals, and consider helping out yourself from time to time. Delegation does not mean avoiding drudgery, it simply means working more effectively.

Researching and collecting information
Collecting and presenting information and calculating data are tasks frequently that take up a great deal of time but rarely require your skills.

Meetings
Consider delegating team members to attend certain meetings on your behalf. This will probably work best for those meetings where team members may openly represent you and actively participate. After the meeting team members can relay important issues to you.

Future responsibilities
Delegate tasks that develop the skills of your team members, or that will be part of the team members' future responsibilities. It is important to remember that by developing your team you will be able to delegate more, and with greater certainty, increasing the success and dynamism of your team.

Tasks which are more cost-effectively completed by
It is always worth considering whether the tas
doing is the best use of your time, asking your
question 'is this what they pay me for?' Delegate tasks
which could be more cost-effectively performed by a
member of your team.

Delegation tip

Before delegating work you need to be sure that your
team members:

- have the necessary skills and authority to complete
  the task successfully
- have available all the information for decision-
  making that they will need
- focus on the right part of the task

What to avoid delegating
It is vital to understand that there are some tasks that
cannot be delegated. Each individual needs to consider
their own job and decide which tasks they must do
themselves. In choosing areas of work to delegate you must
act with discretion. A good rule of thumb is to avoid the
following general areas:

1 *Policy-making and goal setting* – these are key areas for
  managers to focus on and not usually delegated.
2 *Specific people management issues* – discipline,
  appraisal, dispute resolution are also best dealt with by
  managers.
3 *Major external issues* – crisis management or legal
  action.

There are certain activities that normally only someone with the status of a manager can undertake. You should *always* avoid delegating the following tasks:

Delegation

Don't assign the delegation process to someone else. Quite apart from looking lazy or remote it can inevitably lead to communication errors. You should always explain work that is to be completed by your team.

Coaching, counselling and morale issues

Counselling a team member whose attitude is unacceptable is a difficult management task: it needs to be completed by the manager in private, in confidence, and cannot generally be delegated.

Appraisals, performance evaluations and feedback

Performance evaluations and appraisals are a managerial responsibility: they are vital to improving quality, achieving objectives and developing the individual's skills and confidence. It is also important that the same person who delegated them evaluates the tasks. This ensures that the

objectives and standards that should have been mutually
agreed have been met, and that any other issues or
questions are resolved.

Disciplinary proceedings
Disciplinary actions are an unpleasant but necessary aspect
of a manager's job. When they arise they cannot be
avoided. Passing them on to someone else only reduces the
effectiveness of the message and the authority of the
manager. Furthermore, disciplining a team member should
always be done in private and only after all the facts are
known.

Confidential tasks and sensitive situations
It is important not to delegate activities involving sensitive
or classified information (such as salaries), unless it is a
specific part of the person's job. This can put both the
manager and the team member in an awkward position
with colleagues. When dealing with confidential tasks the
manager should either:

- perform them without delegating
- delegate to an appropriate individual, or
- divide the task into segments so that the whole is not
  recognised

Planning and management
The manager's job is to ensure that the team or department
meets the overall aims of the organisation. The views of
team members can, and should, be sought, and research
can also be completed by others; but goal-setting,
department planning and overall management cannot be
delegated.

Complex situations

The manager should know how involved a situation is, and thus be able to avoid delegating confusing or highly involved tasks. Delegating a complex or poorly understood task is ineffective, resulting in a need for constant clarification and advice from the manager.

Tasks which have been specifically assigned

If your manager has deliberately assigned a specific task to you then it is wrong to delegate that task to someone else.

Overcoming problems when preparing to delegate

Adequate preparation is vital for successful delegation. Many difficulties arise because managers take a simplistic view of delegation, seeing it as no more than asking 'will you do this job for me?'

Common problems when preparing to delegate include:

Delegating the wrong type of task
If you don't consider carefully what it is that you are asking your colleagues to do, how and when they will do it and how successful they are likely to be, then you are taking a huge risk. Think clearly about the task first, make sure it can be delegated and consider any other implications (for example, how will other colleagues view it, both inside and outside your team?).

Delegating without planning, preparation or sufficient time
If you don't systematically plan what you are and are not going to delegate then confusion can easily result. Tasks may be delegated incorrectly, to the wrong person, and often come back to the manager, unfinished and worse off than at the start. Time and stress pressures may build up, trust may be reduced and the manager may not be able to find someone to do the job. Think carefully about delegating tasks, and set time aside to delegate properly. It may take time but it saves more.

Only delegating unpleasant tasks
The quickest way to lose respect and authority as a manager is to only delegate boring, trivial or unpleasant tasks, while at the same time saving the enjoyable or visible tasks. Assignments should include both enjoyable and unpleasant tasks, equally divided among team members according to skills, abilities and fairness.

Overlapping tasks and responsibilities
Problems can arise when two or more individuals are responsible for doing the same task. This often means that work assignments are too general or that different jobs have overlapping responsibilities. Quite apart from being inefficient it is usually very annoying and frustrating to the people involved. The solution is to clearly define who does what, specifically outlining responsibilities; if necessary, it may also help to get those involved together to agree who will do what.

Summary

Knowing how to delegate is fine, but without the right attitude and approach your efforts will probably not succeed. Do not be reluctant to delegate: if you are it will hold you back, whereas if you allow yourself to let go of some of your work then you will unburden yourself, releasing your energies for other tasks.

It is also vitally important that you believe in people and trust them to do a good job. You need to give them unwavering support and if you take this approach people will respond: they will find that their skills are being appreciated and feel that their role is important.

It is worth reflecting on your attitude to delegating and answering the following questions:

- Do you make a real effort to let go?
- Are you prepared to trust people?
- Do you always keep your word?
- Do you fully support people when difficulties arise?
- Do you feel that you get other people's commitment?
- Do you encourage people to treat the task as their own?
- Do you have a positive approach to delegating?

Tomorrow we will look at how to match the person you are delegating to with the task that needs to be completed, and how and when to delegate your authority.

Matching person and task: delegating with authority

Getting the right people to do the right job is one of the most important skills in effective management and delegation. Once you have prepared for delegation and decided what tasks to delegate, the next step is to consider who is the best person to do them.

There are several factors affecting selection of the right person for an assignment:

- skills and abilities
- interest
- workload

Matching person to task is not generally the biggest or hardest aspect of delegation, but it is certainly one of the most important.

Analysing people

Choosing the right person to complete a particular task
requires you to analyse their capabilities, and also to
understand what might interest and challenge them. You
will also need to understand how busy they are now and in
the future – their workload.

Skills and abilities
It is important to have an understanding of the capabilities
of each person in your team, how they work with others
and what they do best. This means knowing something of
their training and experience: if the job is too difficult then
frustration and disaster can result, but if it is too simple for
the individual then it is likely to bore and frustrate just the
same, with similar consequences.

Points to consider:

- Make sure you know your team members' abilities – look
  at their record on similar assignments
- Do you know everything that your team members really
  do? This is vital in understanding what they can achieve;
  and it may be that they are already doing it!
- With new and potential employees find out their work
  record, and don't be afraid to ask what they enjoy and
  what they don't; where they succeed and where they find
  things difficult
- How well does the candidate work under pressure?
- How well do they work with others?
- When does the person work at their best?
- Is there any aspect of the task that will prove a difficulty
  for the person?

- If there is no one that can complete the task then consider training:
  - Who could be trained?
  - How long would the training take?
  - What is the best form of training (a course, secondment, discussion with someone else that may have completed it)?

Delegation tip

As a general rule, first consideration should be given to someone who is highly interested in and motivated by the task. Motivation and desire are at least as important as a person's ability.

Team members' motivation
Points to consider:

- Do you know the interests and goals of people in your team?
- Don't be afraid to discuss the task with your team to see their reaction. If they are keen, fine, but even if they are reluctant at least they will have contributed to the process, made their feelings known, and will be more willing to accept the delegation when it occurs.
- Do you know how to treat the people in your team? How to give them each task, agree requirements and follow up with monitoring and evaluation? Simply treating everyone the same way may not be enough: you will almost certainly need different approaches taking into account each person's individual motivations. Do you know what words will encourage, inspire and motivate, and which will cause apprehension and concern?

Points to consider:

- How much extra time is available for the person that you have in mind?
- How much work is the person currently doing?
- Is time a factor in the success, or otherwise, of the person's achievements?
- How does the person's workload compare to that of others in the team?
- How time-sensitive is the task that you are asking to be completed? Is this realistic?
- Consider how long the task should take. If anyone else is involved (e.g. a colleague) then make sure that they know how long you expect the task to take to complete.
- Make sure you keep to time constraints: don't let the work expand to fill the time available!

Understanding people

In some circumstances where you might be managing a large number of people, or where the task being assigned is particularly significant, it is worth preparing a person specification. This is the same sort of approach that people take when interviewing someone for a job: write down the skills and qualities that they need in one column, with another column for each short-listed candidate. Then simply evaluate each person against each quality, perhaps on a scale of 1 to 10. The person with the highest score wins!

This works well in certain situations, and can be useful as a 'tie-breaker' when you have to decide between two or more similar candidates, but on the whole it is better to have a good appreciation of people, keeping in mind their capabilities. This allows routine, easy and instinctive delegation.

In general, people fall into four (or possibly more!) categories when you are delegating.

1 *Stars*
These are accomplished, reliable and experienced people who should be left to get on with the task once it has been delegated. With *Stars*, the best approach is to let them complete things in their own way, and if they ask for help then this request should be taken very seriously. Either things were not explained correctly in the first place, the task is inappropriate, or else the manager failed to match person and task. These people are a huge asset but this demands recognition and respect – anything else will probably cause irritation or frustration.

2   *Comets*

These people are experienced and successful, but they may need support and encouragement from time to time. Their progress should be quietly monitored and they should be encouraged but, again, treated with respect for the talent, attitude and expertise that they bring.

3   *Nebula*

These are inexperienced people who will need to be told how to do the task, but it is worth considering them if they can learn quickly and build confidence. It is particularly important to recognise these people: they may lack experience and confidence, but they do not necessarily lack ability. In time and with active support and encouragement they can become a vital asset – a *Star.*

4   *Pulsars*

Pulsars do not shine bright and tend to be hidden, quietly forgotten. They may not be considered for many delegated tasks but possessing specific skills such as steadiness or the ability to complete urgent tasks, they are invaluable when the need arises.

It is also worth remembering that there may also be *black holes:* people who can cause immense pressure and pull you in different directions! All you need to do is find out where their talents lie, what they enjoy and do well, and then play to their strengths. As confidence and experience grows so will the range of tasks they complete and the success they achieve.

Assessing your team

It is vital that you know and understand the people in your team. In particular, for each member of your team ask yourself:

- what they can do
- what they do best
- how they work
- what they enjoy and dislike
- how much support they need, and when
- how and when to monitor their work
- whether they could improve with training

Understanding people's abilities, their strengths and weaknesses, will ensure that you not only give the right person the right task, but that you also provide the right level of assistance to make the task work well.

Delegation tip

You should also remember that even when you are overwhelmed with a wide range of tasks there is usually someone who can help and provide you with support. You simply need to know who they are and how to ask them!

IS THERE ANYBODY OUT THERE?

Matching tasks to people

Art or science?
There are a number of ways of matching task to people,
and to a large extent the right technique depends on the
scale and complexity of the task as much as the attitude of
the manager. Some people will always delegate and assign
work on the basis of intuition, or possibly just reflex.
Others always take a scientific view, listing criteria and
scoring people against particular qualities and
requirements. Both approaches are right and the effective
manager is the one that develops their own style of
delegating which is routine, appropriate, comfortable and
effective for all involved.

Checklist: getting the right person
Key questions to consider when deciding who to delegate
to are:

1 What exactly does the job involve, and are there any
  specific problem areas?
2 Who would expect to do the job – does it 'belong' to a
  person or position?
3 Who is trained to do the job?
4 Who has the interest and ability to complete the task?
5 Who would benefit from the experience of completing the
  task?
6 Who is available?
7 Who has been neglected in the past? (And who is least
  busy now?)
8 Would the task help anyone to improve their ability for a
  new position or promotion?

Delegation charts

It is often useful to prepare a list of the tasks and people in a *delegation chart*, especially for complex situations and tasks with a large number of variables. There are a number of popular approaches, all with slightly different purposes and emphases, and you may well wish to devise your own.

A typical *delegation matrix* will help decide *what* is being delegated and *who* to. Headings include:

- key areas
- results required/critical issues
- candidates for the task
- strengths/weaknesses
- task assigned to

Delegating with authority

Asking someone to complete a task without giving them the necessary authority to act on your behalf makes it unlikely that the task will be done successfully. This is because the team member will lack the power to obtain and use the resources they need, including:

- access to support staff
- access to information
- respect and understanding that will release expertise and knowledge from others

In many cases the team member will therefore fail to complete the task on time – or just fail completely.

Delegation tip

Authority makes the person grow, both in stature and confidence in themselves, and can be vital to the person successfully completing the task. Delegating a task therefore means delegating the authority to complete it.

Remember that you are granting authority for the team member to take independent action, making decisions and solving problems *for the period in which the task is being completed*.

Defining the level of authority
It is always worth stretching and challenging someone, but if you are unsure about the risks of delegation (perhaps when delegating to someone for the first time) then define the level of authority that you are granting. Generally, there are three levels of authority:

1 No authority
Characteristics:

- you decide the team member's role and responsibilities, and you set the goals, decide how the task should be completed and exactly what the standards should be for completing the task
- you clearly communicate to the team member, in detail, what you expect
- the team member reports regularly to you on progress
- the team member refers any problems or issues that arise to you

When to give this level of authority:
Only very occasionally, or in exceptional circumstances, as it can usually indicate a low level of trust and confidence. If a team member cannot be given some authority then it is important to address the reasons why: it could be a sign of a bigger or more significant problem.

However, there are certain circumstances where you might want to delegate but still assume all authority yourself:

- if the task is unusual, difficult or sensitive
- if the person is new to the task
- if it is a new type of task
- if you have doubts that the task will be completed successfully otherwise (perhaps if the person is leaving the company)

2 **Limited authority**
Characteristics:

- you decide the team member's responsibilities, and together with the person you set the goals, decide the plan of action and the required standards
- the team member consults with you regularly on progress
- the team member consults with you on difficult problems that may arise

When to give this level of authority:
This level of authority works best in complicated, sensitive or important areas where you have complete faith in the ability of the team member, but want to provide them with direct support.

3 **Total authority**
Characteristics:

- you jointly agree the team member's responsibilities
- the team member sets their own goals, plans, performance standards and then acts on them
- the team member keeps you regularly informed of progress
- the team member consults with you on difficult problems only if they think it is necessary
- your role is to guide, support and mentor the team member, helping out only when asked and usually in exceptional circumstances

When to give this level of authority:
This level of authority should be regarded as the standard: the situation to achieve with each team member for every task or project.

You should choose a level of authority when delegating and make clear the amount of authority and latitude the team members are being given.

Summary

Getting the best match between person and task is vitally important when delegating, and while it can be difficult at first it becomes easier with experience, the more you know about what people can do and what each task involves.

When you delegate it is worth remembering:

- To assess the capabilities of each person individually
- What motivates people, what they like and each person's workload
- Whether people are *Stars, Comets, Nebula* or *Pulsars:* this will help you decide *what* to delegate, *how* to delegate work, *who* should receive it and the *level of authority* to give
- To be clear about the level of authority you are giving the person
- To be clear about what you expect the person to do and, if relevant, how you expect the task to be completed. Are there key points or milestones? Do you expect the person to update you regularly? Who deals with problems? When must it be completed?

This requires preparation and planning before delegating, and clear communication when you do delegate. Tomorrow we will look at how to communicate clearly and effectively: briefing team members, agreeing goals and handing over the task.

Communicating with clarity

Having decided what needs to be delegated, who is doing it and how much authority they have, you now need to brief the person – or people – that will complete the task.

This means that you will need to:

- Explain the situation and set the scene
- Set goals
- Communicate responsibilities
- Agree performance measures (standards for completing the job)
- Provide authority
- Establish methods for monitoring, reviewing and evaluating

This process is at the core of successful delegation and includes all the key steps. I call it, quite inappropriately, by its acronym: **ESCAPE.** I should emphasise that ESCAPE means delegating so that you move the whole team forward to achieve the desired objectives: it is not an excuse to dump all the work and run away!

Before we look at briefing the person receiving the task, it is important to understand how to communicate clearly and effectively.

Communication and influencing skills: a checklist

Effective communication is fundamental to good delegation, and there are a number of valuable points to remember when communicating and influencing people:

- *Stop talking* – it is very hard to listen while you talk! And when you delegate you need to listen and understand your team members' reactions, views and concerns
- *Summarise* – give an overview at the start of what you want to say, and finish by summarising what has been agreed. Summarising at key intervals will also help to prevent misunderstandings
- *Empathise* – when you delegate, try to put yourself in the other person's position
- *Signal for attention* – let the other person know if you want to comment and respond to their point, allowing them to pause and switch their attention to you before you speak
- *Question* – asking questions not only improves your understanding but it can also test assumptions and show that you are listening
- *Don't interrupt, embarrass or be rude*
- *Focus on what your team member is really saying, not what you think they are saying*
- *Remember to look out for body language* – this is important, both yours and theirs. Keeping eye contact shows trust and interest, and observing their posture will give some idea of how they feel. Mirroring back someone's body language sensitively is one way of helping to show that you are listening

- *Control your emotions* – leave behind your own fears, problems, and don't get angry at what might be said: stay in control
- *Remove distractions*
- *Listen for how things are said, and what is not said*
- *Be critically aware* – this means reacting to ideas, not people; focusing on the significance to the discussion of the facts and evidence; avoiding jumping to conclusions
- *Avoid quick decisions* – give yourself time to think and react
- *Understand yourself* – recognise your own views and prejudices and avoid letting them influence your behaviour

Remember, if you disagree with what is being said don't start by saying that you disagree: this can often prompt a defensive or negative response. Instead, outline your views first and then explain why you disagree.

Delegation tip

Remember that delegation can involve an element of negotiation: you need to be prepared to listen and understand the other person's views and concerns, and act on them.

Explain the situation and set the scene

When you brief the team member you should set the scene. This usually involves explaining several key points:

1 *What you want doing* – for example, 'I want you to work out the costs for developing this new marketing campaign.'

2 *Why it is important and needs to be done* – 'We need to
   start generating new sales leads and clients for the
   autumn.'
3 *How it fits into the overall work or function of the team* –
   'This campaign fits into our overall strategy of
   broadening the number of clients we have, and getting
   more clients internationally.'
4 *Why you have chosen them* – the next step is to gain
   your team member's commitment by personalising the
   task and explaining why you have confidence in their
   ability to do the work. 'You were particularly successful in
   organising the marketing campaign earlier in the year.'
   Or, 'You know what is required and have the skills to do it
   really well.'

It is important that you get their response by asking open
questions, e.g. 'How do you feel about this?' This way you
will not only assess their commitment and attitude, but you
should also be able to uncover any concerns that they may
have, and then reassure them.

Delegation tip

Don't be afraid to give people background information
about the task that they are completing: it is vital that
people know what to expect as well as what to do.

Set goals

You need to agree what the outcome should be, and set
goals that are SMART:

Specific – don't just tell the person to complete a job; specify what you are looking for and any alternatives that may be relevant.

Measurable – goals should be observable and measurable. In the above example, simply saying 'We need to watch our marketing costs for future campaigns' may be good advice, but if the person can't measure it then it can't be managed properly.

Attainable – the best goals are those that are stretching and challenging but achievable.

Results related (also *Realistic* and *Relevant*)– when setting goals you should keep them simple and focused. There may be a lot to do, and completing the task may open up other opportunities, but you need to focus your team member to concentrate on those goals that are important to completing the overall task.

Time-constrained – you should not be afraid to exert a little pressure, either by setting challenging goals or pushing for a shorter time frame. This is a powerful means of focusing attention and effort, and also avoiding the task expanding simply to fill the time available! However, remember that too much pressure is counter-productive, resulting in stress and mistakes.

Delegation tip

Be clear and focused about the outcome that you expect, and let your team members plan their own way of tackling the assignment.

Communicate responsibilities

You need to ensure that *both* you and your team members understand the responsibilities they are assuming. Once you are clear about the goals that need to be achieved it is quite straightforward to agree responsibilities. Using the example that we mentioned before, the manager might say, 'I would like the report on marketing costs to be completed by the end of this week, and delivered to me and the finance department. Also, highlight any areas where we might be able to reduce costs further.'

Bear in mind that responsibilities can be:

- written or oral
- formal or informal
- specific or general.

Delegation tip

Remember that the more specific the responsibilities are, the greater the likelihood of the task being completed as intended.

Agree performance measures (standards for completing the job)

It is vitally important that you let the team member know what good performance is when you hand over the task. The advantage of setting performance measures is that they provide a means of monitoring and evaluating performance, enabling you to measure how well the task is progressing. For the team member they can act as guidelines in completing the task.

There are a number of points to remember when setting performance measures and these include:

Quality standards – you and the team member must agree on standards of quality. You both need to be clear about what constitutes excellent, acceptable and poor quality.

Resourcing – you need to agree the parameters within which the task must be completed. In particular, how much time, money or other resources will be required.

Deliverables – it helps to be as specific as possible about what you expect to see at the end of the task.

Measuring performance

You need to agree with the team member how you will measure their performance. Measurements should be simple, easy to apply and understand; reliable and consistent; objective and fair. For example, if you are a sales manager responsible for a team of salesmen then you might agree the number of potential new customers they contact; the number of quotations they generate and the level of business they attain. It is important to try to avoid changing performance measures, or to do so only by agreement, as this implies that you are moving the target (and making it harder for it to be hit!).

Performance can be measured in a variety of ways, both formal and informal, but perhaps the best method is through observation and discussion: what seems to be happening? How are people reacting and how is the task being perceived?

You should also be sensitive to the way people sound and behave: if the team member is chain-smoking, irritable and staying at the office until midnight then it might be a sign that things have – or will soon – go wrong!

Provide authority

Delegating authority is vitally important to achieving success. It means giving the person completing the task the authority to spend money, represent you and the organisation, and seek assistance from others. It affects their level of confidence and ultimately their success.

You should always delegate some measure of authority when you delegate; if not, how will the task be completed? Look at it from the team member's perspective: what does it say to the person doing the task that you are not prepared to grant them any authority?

Delegation tip

The amount of authority that you grant has a huge effect on the decisions and approach that the team member takes.

Authority can be defined as the permission to act on your behalf. In effect you are granting authority for independent action and decision-making until the task is completed, but beware! Once given, delegated authority can be difficult to get back. It is best to delegate authority and expect the person to keep it: that way they can complete the task the next time it arises, at the same time building confidence, esteem and motivation.

You should follow the following guidelines when delegating authority:

- delegate the right level of authority necessary to complete the task (the level may vary between tasks)
- make clear to the team member the level of authority they have – check understanding and make sure that they agree
- if necessary, reassure the team member
- don't avoid the issue – it could cause confusion and problems later

As far as possible you should be explicit about what they are authorised to do, and if necessary where they do not have authority.

Delegation tip

Attitude and trust are everything. Think positive.

Establish methods for monitoring, reviewing and evaluating

At the end of the briefing session it is essential that you agree how you will monitor and support the person doing the task. This is your opportunity to reassure them that you are available to mentor, guide and support them; and also to let them know how and when you will be monitoring their progress. Some managers avoid doing this, fearful that it will look like interference and meet with resistance. In reality this is not the case – most people expect and value a framework in which to report progress, successes and any difficulties they may encounter.

Summary

Listening
When you communicate you should remember that listening is at least as important as telling. This will help to make you aware of any difficulties, concerns or potential problems early on so that you can make sure they are addressed.

Negotiating

You should also be prepared to discuss, negotiate and agree aspects of the task with your team member. Remember that you are looking to gain their commitment, initiative and enthusiasm, and this is more likely to happen if you start giving them some authority and influence from the start.

Hands off

Once you have briefed the team member and agreed what you expect and what the reporting system will be, you then need to step back and let the person get on with it. It is also worth remembering that people will almost certainly do the task differently to you, and that it may even be better. As long as the performance measures are met and the task is achieved then that is a success.

Rewards

As well as the steps involved in ESCAPE, some people believe that when communicating and delegating the task the manager should also establish rewards. This may be appropriate for certain tasks and certain situations, and it is certainly worth considering, but I am not a fan of either carrots or sticks! Rewards should normally be linked to overall performance and not the completion of a single task or project.

Remember, when communicating a task you should:

- set the scene and give relevant background information so that the person can do the job
- make sure that people understand what is required
- jointly discuss and agree what the task requires (rather than dictating or imposing your will)
- be positive and show confidence in your team member's ability
- define the standards required (the performance measures)
- mentor, coach and encourage when needed
- agree a process for regular communication, including how and when you will monitor, review and evaluate
- make sure that the person knows how much authority they have
- check that the team member has the necessary skills and resources to complete the task.
- brief the person well enough to hand over the task completely – and then don't interfere or worry!

Tomorrow we will look at techniques for overcoming problems when delegating.

Overcoming problems when delegating

Delegating effectively can be like running a hurdle race – over a marathon course! However the prizes at the end are worth the effort: success, productivity, enjoyment, progress and profit. As with any race, effective delegation starts with preparing well in advance, making successful completion much more likely.

If each of the stages outlined in the previous chapters is followed then the chances of things going wrong will be greatly reduced, but remember that every situation and every person is different. At each key stage of the process there are potential pitfalls! Fortunately there are a number of common sense techniques that can be used to overcome problems when delegating and these are reviewed today. They include:

- recognising problems
- developing the right attitudes (both yours and theirs)
- monitoring, reviewing and evaluating progress
- problem-solving

Recognising problems

Recognising potential pitfalls when delegating is the first step in preventing them. If this fails, then emergency plan B is to face them head-on and deal with them quickly and effectively. Both require you to know a problem when you see it, and when delegating they can often be well hidden.

Danger signals: signs that delegation may not be working

- Team members are always too busy
- Low morale
- Excessive arguments and 'political' difficulties, either within your team or between teams
- Productivity declines
- Mistakes increase
- Deadlines are not being met
- Team members are frequently surprised by your actions: what you are doing and what you expect of them
- Team members resist tasks
- Team members keep asking for your advice and help
- Worrying comments from others (e.g. customers, your boss or other people in the organisation)
- Team members question their role, or worry excessively about their competence
- Team members leave (or worse, they ask for more money!)

This is by no means an exhaustive list and it is important to be sensitive to signs that things are not going well. Also, you need to remember that some of these may well occur from time to time anyway: what matters is *how often they arise* and *how long they stay* – too much is a problem.

Delegation tip

Always make sure that you promote an atmosphere of trust and openness: this will prove invaluable not only in preventing problems but in tackling them early, positively, and finding the best solution.

Making it happen: developing the right attitudes

An ability to motivate people is an essential management skill, and obtaining commitment from team members is a vital part of overcoming problems. Without doubt the greatest level of success is achieved when teams are fully committed to the task, using each other's abilities and skills to accomplish their goals. However, both commitment and motivation need to be developed through active involvement - they cannot be forced. Active involvement and authority develops a sense of personal ownership, and it is at this stage that people are giving their best.

You will obtain commitment from people when you convince them that:

- the task is necessary, worthwhile and contributes to the organisation as a whole
- they have the necessary authority to act and they are expected to deliver the results themselves. This way they can respond to the challenge but also enjoy the satisfaction completing the task in their own way
- you believe they can do it, increasing their self-confidence and their openness to the task

Monitoring, evaluating and reviewing progress

Delegation is no substitute for your active interest and support: it is essential that you keep your team on the right track by preparing, communicating, monitoring and providing feedback.

Delegation tip

Delegation is not about leaving someone else to do the work that you have no time to do yourself and forgetting about it. It is about getting the job done, and making sure that it is being done well.

Effective monitoring

Successfully monitoring someone to whom you have delegated work is like walking a tightrope: you can either fall off and start interfering, or fall the other way and not monitor enough, becoming out of touch. To stay on course you need to do two things:

1 Agree with the team member when they will update you on progress, if necessary agreeing where the key points or milestones are.
2 Keep open the communication channels so that you are aware of any problems.

Remember that people should be monitored in different ways depending on each particular task, individual and situation. Constant chivvying along the lines of 'How are you doing?' 'How are you doing *now*?' 'Still going OK?' is likely to irritate most people more than anything, draining away their enthusiasm. As well as treating other people as you would wish to be treated, remember to treat people as individuals. Some people will need checking only on completion; some at agreed review points, and others by careful probing during the task. This can be done by finding out how the task is being completed and comparing:

- what should be happening
- what is actually happening
- whether the degree of variation between the two is of concern

Taking action

If things do seem to be going wrong the next step is to discuss things calmly with the team member: it is still their task and it should remain so. The manager should focus on helping the team member to find a solution that everyone is happy with.

> ### Delegation tip
>
> You should always try to avoid interfering and taking direct control of a task that has been delegated. Instead, provide support and encourage the team member to develop and implement their own solution.

Remember the adages that there is no point having a dog and barking yourself, and there is no point trying to catch your own tail!

Your response should depend on the extent of the problem. The first thing to do is to arrange a meeting to check whether there is a problem at all. The advantage of regular reviews or update sessions is that this can be done quite routinely, and you may find that things are under control after all.

Advising and avoiding reverse delegation
It is usually at this point in the task that things can revert back to you, sometimes with you and the team member unaware that this is happening! This is reverse or upward delegation. To keep things on track you should reflect questions back to the team member, helping them to find their answers: this way they will still have ownership of and enthusiasm for the task, bringing a successful outcome much nearer.

Reviewing and providing feedback
When the task or assignment is completed you should always review with your team member how it went, making sure that points are made and any lessons are learnt. This not only benefits you and the individual, but the team and the organisation as a whole.

When reviewing a task you should:

- be positive, celebrate success and congratulate the person for things that went well
- compare the outcome with the performance standards that were set at the start and discuss how things went
- check the team member's perception: what have they learnt?
- identify areas for improvement

In general, a feedback session is an opportunity to consolidate learning in a blame-free way, enabling team members to recognise their own achievements and build their confidence.

Problem-solving

There are a number of steps to follow, or to encourage your team to follow, when solving problems:

1 *Define the problem* – ask the questions what, when, where and who? Remember what you are trying to achieve – go back to first principles – and see how much difficulty the problem is causing.
2 *Gather relevant information* – don't be put off by distractions and ask: what is the problem? what is affected by the problem? who is affected by it? who is not affected by it?
3 *Identify possible causes* – these may relate to people, systems or equipment.
4 *Identify a possible solution* – remember that you are not only treating the symptoms, you need to get to the root of the problem and tackle the causes of the problem.
5 *Check the solution, consider other possible options* – imagine how the solution will work in practice, where it might fail, and adjust it if necessary. Assess the likely consequences of the solution. Also, consider other solutions and actions: action may be needed in a number of areas.
6 *Make the decision* – select the promising solution, plan its implementation and then stick with it! Beware of avoiding a decision, this will only result in losing control.

7   *Monitor the results* – monitor the effects of the solution and make any adjustments that are needed.

A guide to trouble-free delegation

Potential problems	Possible solutions
Problems when preparing to delegate	
1. Inadequate planning leading to work being done wrongly, by the wrong person or not at all.	With major projects and tasks it is always worth taking time to plan the delegation. Even when you routinely delegate work it is still worth from time to time reviewing how you delegate, when and to whom. Set aside sufficient time to delegate properly.
2. 'Dustbin' delegation – only giving rotten, difficult or unappealing tasks.	Team members will quickly lose respect if this situation continues. Remember that tasks should be fairly assigned on the basis of people's abilities and interests, and you should ensure that no one person is suffering unfairly.
3. Not making boundaries and areas of responsibility clear.	Conflict can frequently arise when more than one person is responsible for the same task. This is generally caused by assignments being too general,

or jobs not being clearly defined. The solutions are:

- specifically outline roles and responsibilities
- ensure that those involved decide who will do what.

Problems when delegating

4. Failing to delegate authority.

A common complaint, this can be prevented by:

- reviewing the tasks involved and providing the necessary authority
- checking with the team member to make sure they have the right level of authority.

5. Delegating without sufficient explanation, agreement or commitment.

This is both ineffective and unfair: it will cause confusion and reluctance and is best avoided. Ask the person whether you have provided enough information after you have made the assignment.

6. Structuring and planning the execution in too much detail.

This is another real demotivator that robs the team member of challenge, interest, and achievement. You should:

- promote initiative
- focus on what needs to be done, not how to do it

This in turn will increase the quality of the work done, and the amount that the team member learns from it.

7. Unrealistic delegation: too much required too soon.

Remember that delegating does not mean losing touch with your team, nor does it remove you from your responsibilities as a manager. Focus on the task to be done, resources available and the person completing it. Agree with the team member what is needed then let them deliver.

8. Reverse – or upward – delegation, that means you end up doing the task.

This frequently arises when a team member asks for information or help: the manager then tries to provide it themselves and in the process ends up doing the task. The solutions are:

- to clearly define who the problem belongs to before agreeing to help – if it is the team member's then suggest what *they* might do, rather than doing it yourself
- to make sure you do not work on the delegated activity without the team member.

The team member must complete the task: the manager's job is to coach, support and encourage.

9. Putting undue pressure on people

Often it can be difficult to assess whether enough pressure is too much: knowing the individual and remaining sensitive is one solution. Another important point is to remain accessible, and to foster a 'no-blame' environment so that people can own up to problems, rather than hide them, ignore them or make them worse.

Problems when monitoring,
evaluating and reviewing
delegation

10. Intervening, interfering and undermining

What is worse than not having adequate authority is being told you have the authority, then finding out that you don't! You should make sure that you are consistent and reliable: if you do make a mistake, for instance giving too much authority, then be open and honest in dealing with the situation – and don't repeat it!

11. Too little or too much control

Experience will show how closely, if at all, you need to monitor team members. Also, always try to give the person enough space and trust to complete the task themselves. Be accessible, providing advice and support if needed.

12. Correcting or finishing off delegated tasks.

Beware of being a perfectionist and seeking improvements that are not necessary. This, together with constant criticism, interference, doing or redoing a delegated task, is hugely frustrating. If you have reason to be genuinely worried then the solutions are:

- to adjust the amount of authority the team member has
- to agree review stages with the team member, and use these as an opportunity to guide the individual.

13. Not reviewing tasks properly.

This can often lead to misunderstandings later. Reviewing performance is a valuable step in improving future performance: it highlights strengths, weaknesses and things that need to change – it is vital!

14. Not rewarding performance.

Commitment, quality and performance in general will rapidly decline if team member's efforts are not recognised and rewarded. Thank people, give credit where it is due and make sure that your team is rewarded appropriately for their successes.

Summary

Preparation and developing the right attitudes, both
yourself and within your team, are vital in preventing
problems when delegating. Common-sense management is
needed to overcome difficulties if they do arise.

Remember, it is best to avoid problems by preparing to:

- delegate the right type of task
- match the best person with each task
- plan and prepare the delegation briefing
- avoid only delegating unpleasant tasks
- make sure there is no confusion about overlapping roles

Delegation will work better if:

- you monitor progress without interfering, and in your own
  mind compare what is happening with what should
  happen
- you resolve problems early, and encourage others to face
  them too by instilling a 'blame free' approach in your
  team
- you help people to overcome any difficulties, ideally by
  encouraging them to find their own solutions (if they are
  the people closest to the problem then they will probably
  have the best idea about how to solve it)
- you review how the assignment was performed, drawing
  lessons for the future and providing feedback to the team
  member
- you give fair recognition and reward for successes

Tomorrow we will look at how delegation relates to other
key management skills, and how they can help you
delegate and manage more effectively.

Delegation and other key management skills

Delegation is a vitally important, central management skill. As we have seen, it draws on other key skills such as problem-solving and communicating. To delegate effectively, however, requires you to understand and use other core skills when appropriate. These include:

- Mentoring
- Empowerment
- Setting objectives and performance measures
- Preventing and resolving conflict when delegating
- Leadership and team-building

Mentoring

Mentoring can be defined as a process where the manager offers help, guidance and support to facilitate the learning or understanding of another. Mentoring is a key skill when delegating; it is particularly useful as a means of showing your team member that this is their task – and you are here to support if necessary.

The four key qualities of mentors
There are many aspects to successful mentoring but four key qualities are widely recognised as being of special importance:

1 *Relevant work experience* – this includes passing on experience and knowledge of how best to approach the task, and where potential pitfalls lie.

2 *Experience and knowledge of the organisation* –
knowing how to get things done and acting as a gateway
to sources of information and support.
3 *Interpersonal skills* – knowing how to listen to others;
asking questions that are both challenging and reflective.
It is this 'sounding-board' approach that is one of the
most valuable aspects of mentoring and it is essential
when getting a team member to focus on their task –
how to approach it generally and how to solve problems.
4 *Role model* – providing an example that encourages,
motivates and reassures the team member, making it
clear that the task they are trying to achieve is attainable.

Delegation tip

Remember when dealing with team members to
challenge them to find their own solutions – this way
they retain ownership of the idea and enthusiasm,
rather than having to deal with a prescribed solution. It
also forces people to face up to the situation and take

responsibility, rather than having someone else simply bale them out. Make sure that people reflect on the best way forward themselves, perhaps by asking probing, challenging or reflective questions.

Pitfalls for delegators when mentoring or reviewing performance
Inevitably, the qualities of a poor mentor are the same as those of a poor delegator:

- wishing to dominate and prescribing solutions
- being critical and inflexible
- being insensitive and authoritarian – for example, imposing solutions, plans and arbitrary deadlines
- rigidly defending the status quo
- talking, not listening

These can often result from insecurity and it is worth remembering that you as manager have nothing to prove – after all, you are the one giving the work. Also, some of these attitudes may result from a fear of change. This, too, is nothing to be worried about. When you delegate something for the first time that is, in itself, the biggest change. It is almost inevitable that it will be done slightly differently. The answer is to focus on the needs of the task and the individual – what will it take to get the job done? Remember, change and innovation are the only ways to make progress.

Qualities for successful mentoring managers
When delegating, a successful mentoring manager must
have the ability to:

1 give or release responsibility at the right time, in the right
   way
2 realise that there are different ways of doing things –
   each will have its own merits and value
3 encourage others in being creative, innovating and
   working things out for themselves
4 support and encourage personal professional
   development in others
5 provide clear, constructive and unbiased feedback

Empowerment

Empowerment takes delegation one step further: it is a way
of releasing the creative power that your team has, not for
one specific task but in their job as a whole. It is based on
the belief that the full capabilities of team members are
frequently under-used, and given the right work

environment and level of responsibility people will start to make a much greater, positive contribution. In effect, when you empower your team members you are letting them get on with the job *entirely:* they are both responsible and accountable, within certain agreed boundaries.

Empowerment is about:

- letting each member of your team get on with their job
- letting those team members closest to customers (both within and outside the organisation) take decisions themselves
- removing obstacles and unnecessary bureaucracy
- encouraging and enabling people to put their ideas for improvement into practice

If you are keen for your team to develop so that they take a much greater level of responsibility for themselves all the time, working autonomously and putting effective ideas into practice, then the next stage is to move from delegation to empowerment.

Key stages in empowering your team

1 *Understand what you mean by empowerment* – make sure you know what you want to get out of empowering your team; let your colleagues and senior managers know your plans, and check that their expectations meet your own.
2 *Assess the barriers to empowerment* – what are they (for example, staff may fear responsibility, or there may be a bureaucratic or conservative culture that is unreceptive to change), and how can they be overcome?

3 *Build the right culture within your team* – some
   organisations have cultures that are more conducive to
   empowerment than others. If you are serious about
   empowering your team to make their own decisions and
   take greater responsibility then you should promote trust
   and respect; remove a climate of fear and blame, and
   focus on the needs of the task, team and each
   individual.

4 *Establish the boundaries* – empowerment provides staff
   with greater autonomy and responsibility, but it is
   important that you set and agree clear limits. This may
   include referring types of decision, such as agreeing
   expenditure above a certain level, to you. Also, be
   prepared to have these boundaries tested – only then
   will clear limits be established.

5 *Communicate and win support* – you will need to raise
   awareness among those around you of what is involved
   in empowerment: this may involve reassuring some,
   selling the benefits and winning the support of others.

6 *Ensure that your staff have the necessary skills and
   resources to take control* – review what each member of
   your team does now and what they are likely to be doing
   in future. This is an opportunity to alter and update job
   descriptions; assess training needs, and make sure that
   your team has sufficient resources.

7 *Agree objectives and performance measures* –
   empowerment is about giving people the responsibility
   and resources to complete tasks on an ongoing basis.
   As with delegation, it is not about dumping work on
   people and leaving them, and requires you to agree the
   necessary level of speed, accuracy and cost-efficiency.

8 *Launch and support the empowerment initiative, and monitor developments* – once the ground has been prepared empowerment can take effect. You will need to make people aware of what is happening and try to secure early 'wins' and successes that highlight the value of the process. Monitor developments and iron out any difficulties, particularly in the early days, but be sure that you are not interfering or undermining the process!

Remember that when you empower your team members you are giving them a complete *job* and area of responsibility, within definite boundaries, rather than delegating one specific *task* or *project*.

Objective setting and performance measures

When delegating you need to be clear about the objectives of the task or job being done, and communicate them clearly to each team member. It is important to appreciate that objectives need to:

- be specific, so the team member is clear about what is to be achieved
- be measurable, so they know whether they have got there or not
- have clearly defined boundaries in terms of time and cost
- be challenging but attainable
- be discussed and agreed between the manager setting the objective and the team member that will tackle it. Where necessary, compromise and initiative will be required to make sure that progress is made and total commitment is forthcoming

- have clear performance measures against which progress can be assessed

Identifying appropriate performance measures
Performance measures indicate what is expected and how well team members are doing in achieving the task. They must be clear, concise, easy to collect and interpret, and relevant. Performance measures are usually agreed between the manager and team member and there should be a process for regularly reviewing them.

Measures usually relate to:

- *Speed* – how quickly the team member delivers
- *Quality* – how well the work is being done (e.g. how good or accurate was the service provided to the customer)
- *Cost* – how cost-efficiently the task is being completed

Therefore performance measures for delegated tasks might typically cover information relating to:

- finance – both costs and income
- customer satisfaction
- resources – what are being used and what are no longer required
- processes – how efficiently and effectively tasks and activities are being completed

Delegation tip

Agree clear objectives and performance measures that will provide targets showing how well things are going, and where there are areas for further attention.

Preventing and resolving conflict when delegating

In any team or work situation conflicts may arise: this can easily happen when work is delegated, even when there has been careful preparation in advance. There are many possible causes of conflict including *personal clashes* resulting from an argument; a poor relationship or basic personality clash; or a personality defect such as bullying. There are also *professional causes* of conflict. These might arise from different approaches and ways of working; a fear of change; concern or dissatisfaction with some aspect of employment, or office rumours.

Techniques for preventing conflict in the long term
- *Communicate with people regularly* – by maintaining a regular dialogue you will be able to spot conflicts and resentments building up. It will also help you in deciding how, when and to whom you should delegate.

- *Assess the culture and management style of the business* – is it overly aggressive? Is there an atmosphere of intense competition, rivalry or blame? Is it conservative, hierarchical and not open to discussion? You may not be able to change the culture of the business, but by understanding it you can make allowances and build the best team that suits your goals.
- *Encourage teamwork and build team spirit* – if you can instil a sense of common purpose this will reduce the chances of conflict. Encouraging teamwork will also ensure that people are used to working together and increase understanding.
- *Set clear, formal, professional standards* – make people aware of what is acceptable behaviour and what is not. This starts from the interview process onwards!
- *Encourage free communication and an open door policy* – if people feel that they can discuss a particular situation then you are more likely to be able to defuse any potential problems that may develop.

Resolving conflict

If the conflict is personal it is usually best to avoid getting too involved: the manager's role is to limit the effects on the business and make it clear to both people that the job needs to be done. Don't fall into the trap of thinking that management is about making friends! If conflict does arise try some (hopefully not all) of the following approaches:

- *Talk to each person individually* – try to remain neutral, objective and constructive; remain in control and be confident. Let them express their grievances and help them to deal with the problem, perhaps by encouraging them to explore possible solutions themselves, or else deciding the best course of action yourself.

- *Make them face their situation and communicate* – they created the situation, they need to understand that they need to help resolve it. Clear, regular, open communication is a good first step.
- *Consider making them work together* – it may be that the problem could be resolved if each person understood the other, and their situation, better. It may also be that there is no other alternative: they will have to get on so get them to realise the fact and start as they may mean to go on.
- *Remove the problem* – if the difficulty is influenced or exacerbated by an outside cause then consider what action you can take to remove or alleviate the problem.

Leadership and team-building

Sound leadership is a vital aspect of successful delegation. Empowering leaders have the following qualities that influence and underpin the way they delegate:

- they realise the importance of constant learning
- they are willing to challenge the way things are done, supporting innovation and initiative
- they are good communicators with a willingness to ask questions and listen to answers
- they have the capacity to make themselves clearly understood at every level
- leaders have an ability to build sound relationships based on trust, respect and a clear understanding of others
- they handle criticism by listening, drawing out concerns and taking clear, positive action
- they are focused on building people's esteem, confidence, skills and initiative

Delegation tip

Be prepared to challenge the way that things are normally done. Encourage innovation and initiative, and realise that by giving people authority they will take responsibility.

Summary

Effective delegation is based on a number of simple, common-sense ideas that provide the keys to successful management. These include:

- if you give people authority they will take responsibility
- the people closest to the action (meaning the task customer or front-line) know best. Empowerment is about giving power to the people who actually do the job, because they know what is required to achieve success
- if you treat people like robots they will behave like robots

You will be a better delegator if you:

- challenge team members to find their own solutions
- encourage creativity, innovation and initiative
- empower your team so they don't just take responsibility for a task, but for their whole job, constantly making positive improvements
- set clear, challenging objectives
- agree and regularly monitor performance measures
- prevent conflicts arising in the long term
- recognise and deal with conflicts that have arisen
- lead your team and give them a framework that brings out their talents and skills

Tomorrow we will review the key points from the week and look at delegating for the first time.

Delegating for the first time

Delegating is a central management skill and whether one is a first line supervisor, an army commander or the head of a major corporation it will always remain vitally important. Effective delegation is about achieving your goals through others, but it requires much more than simply giving orders and walking away. As we have seen, effective delegation involves several key stages:

- Preparing to delegate
- Matching person to task
- Communicating clearly
- Monitoring, reviewing and evaluating

All the time the manager needs to:

- be sure that the task is being accomplished
- ensure that the conditions are right and that there are sufficient resources
- provide the right level of support, guidance and encouragement
- delegate the right level of authority – ideally as much as possible
- be able to spot difficulties that may arise and then make sure that the team member resolves them

Letting go
If you are concerned about delegating for the first time then I suggest first focusing on the benefits for you, including better use of your time, developing the skills and realising the potential of others, reducing stress and difficulties, achieving more. The main fear for first time delegators is

that they simply will not get the results they want. With careful planning and effective management this certainly need not be the case: it is much more likely that you will get the desired result – or better – albeit by a different method than the one you might choose.

Even if problems do arise the first time do not dismiss delegation. Instead review what happened, where difficulties arose, how they should have been handled and how to act in future. Just as you should encourage your team to review and critically evaluate their actions from time to time, so you should do the same yourself.

Avoiding failure

Studies have shown that there are two main reasons why delegation fails, both relating to people's attitudes. Either delegation fails because people do not want to take on the additional task and responsibility that goes with it; or the manager (consciously or otherwise) wants to keep the responsibility, inevitably undermining the process. Before delegating, check that neither of these is the case, and if either of these attitudes do appear then you will need to tackle and resolve them. Remember, it is not only the team member that can benefit from the advice, perception and support of a mentor – find one that you as a manager can discuss the situation with, usually your boss.

Getting started
As a starting point, draw up a list based on the following simple questions:

1 What tasks can I delegate?
2 What does each task involve?
3 Who can do each task (this may not necessarily be just your team members)?
4 What should I be doing to put people to work?

Now that you know all the tips and techniques for successful delegation it is time to put them to use.

Preparing to delegate – a checklist

Preparing to delegate for the first time
Spend some time thinking about your attitude to delegating:

• Are you positive about delegation? If not, this will probably become known to your team with the risk that their confidence and enthusiasm will disappear.
• Do you avoid delegating because it will take too long? Remember that time invested in delegating is not wasted. Recurring and similar tasks are routinely

completed and new tasks can be given to people who are confident and used to receiving new challenges.

- Do you find it difficult to know which task to start with? Then prioritise your list of tasks – and remember the value of early wins and successes in building confidence.

- Are you unhappy about giving authority and trust to other people? There are a number of possible options here. The first is quite simple – don't trust them, or at least not at first. Instead consider working with them on the task, or structuring it so that you still retain authority. A second option is to be straightforward and open and try to increase the level of trust. A third option is to take a risk, ideally with a little task or a component of a larger assignment.

> ### Delegation tip
> Remember, procrastination takes too much time – take action instead.

Matching person and task so you delegate with authority
Some key points to consider when matching person to task include:

- do you know what the task involves?
- who is reliable, with the right attitude for the task?
- who is prepared to take a risk, if that is required?
- who has the best decision-making and problem-solving skills, as they can frequently be required?
- who will absorb the work with a minimum of fuss or disruption?
- within my team who are the *Stars, Comets, Nebulae* and *Pulsars?*
- what level of authority are you assigning for this task?

Communicating with clarity
Clear communication is an essential component for delegation from the start through to the final review. Before you delegate you might want to consider:

- how much information do you need to provide?
- what reaction do you expect from the team member? do you need to prepare for this reaction?
- what are the best ways of influencing the person doing the task?
- how much training, mentoring or instruction is needed?
- who deals with problems?

- is the team member clear about your expectations? do they know how much authority they have? do you need to check understanding?
- to what extent do you show trust and obtain commitment?
- have you created and made it clear that there is a blame-free environment?

Delegation tip

People respond best to clear and open communication. If you try to be too clever about what you say (or don't say), or avoid giving necessary information, then people may quickly lose respect.

Monitoring, evaluating and controlling delegation
- what are going to be the standards for the job? do you set them or will they be agreed jointly?
- how will you monitor the task and what is the process for reporting progress?
- do you monitor without interfering?
- are you prepared to intervene only if a cataclysmic disaster strikes?
- will you encourage people to arrive at their own solutions to problems?
- has the monitoring and review process been agreed with the team member?
- do you give full credit to people for their work and successes?

Summary

It is worth considering that while most of this book has focused on delegating to team members and people that report to you as a manager, the same skills work when delegating to others, particularly colleagues and suppliers.

A final thought
It is certainly worth reflecting on your own career when preparing to delegate. When did you work most successfully? Who was the most impressive manager you ever worked with – and the least – and what qualities did they have? How did they approach delegation? Individual personality and style are of course vital features affecting how successfully managers delegate: within the framework we have outlined you should look to develop your own style, a way of working that you feel entirely comfortable with. Finally, remember that the more you delegate the easier it becomes and the more successful you will be.